Echoes from the Heart

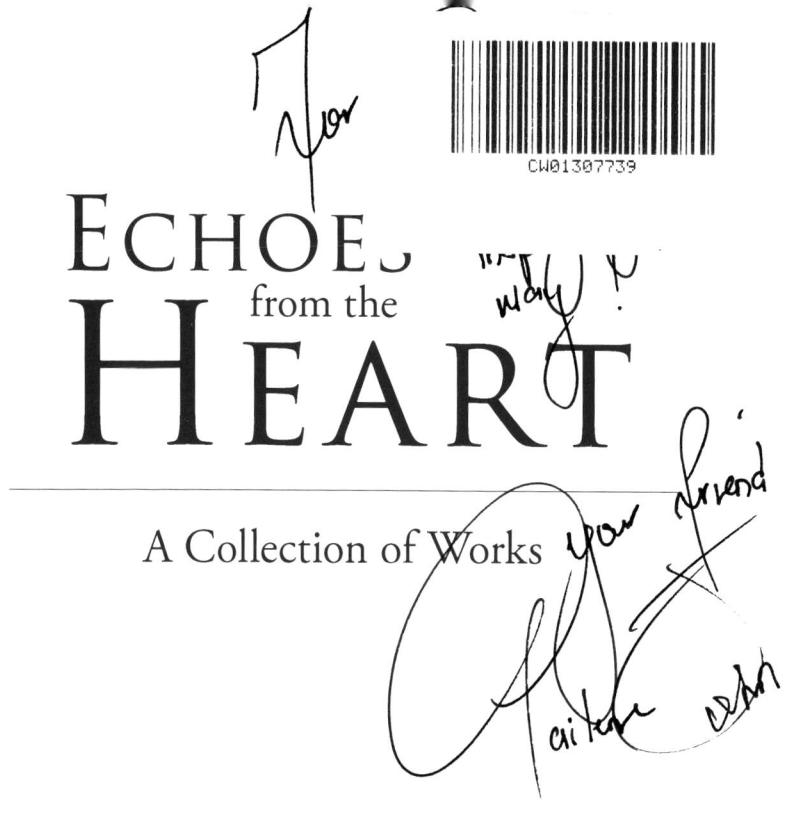

A Collection of Works

GAILENE JOHN

authorHOUSE

AuthorHouse™ UK
1663 Liberty Drive
Bloomington, IN 47403 USA
www.authorhouse.co.uk
Phone: 0800.197.4150

© 2017 Gailene John. All rights reserved.

No part of this book may be reproduced, stored in a retrieval system, or transmitted by any means without the written permission of the author.

Published by AuthorHouse 01/26/2017

ISBN: 978-1-5246-7682-7 (sc)
ISBN: 978-1-5246-7683-4 (e)

Print information available on the last page.

Any people depicted in stock imagery provided by Thinkstock are models, and such images are being used for illustrative purposes only.
Certain stock imagery © Thinkstock.

This book is printed on acid-free paper.

Because of the dynamic nature of the Internet, any web addresses or links contained in this book may have changed since publication and may no longer be valid. The views expressed in this work are solely those of the author and do not necessarily reflect the views of the publisher, and the publisher hereby disclaims any responsibility for them.

Contents

Preface ix
Echoes of a broken heart 1
Light Bulb 2
Fade 3
Play Me 5
What more can I give? 7
Love Me 9
Betrayed 12
State of Mind 13
Colourful passion 14
Dreams 15
Diversity 16
What is love? 18
Absent 20
Chance Meeting 21
Passion 23
Love Torn Tragedy: What If? 25
Windows to the soul 26
Erika: Ode to Dominica 27
Glory Day 33
Journey 35
Nature's Fury Part 1 37
Nature's Glory Part 2 38
Exalt 40

Meditation	41
Flowers for a lady	42
Late Nights	43
Subliminal	44
Second chances	45
Nonsense Poems	46
Dinky the Bat	47
The vagabond cat	48
Life	49
Pain	50
Black Is My Beauty	52
My Room	54
Ballad: Rosie's Demise [AH HUH]	56
Island Life	59
The End of the Road	61

This is for you, Tom. Thanks for always being there for me. For your kindness, unwavering support and devotion in love.

Preface

This is a collection of eclectic poems and inspirational words written over different chapters of my life. It all began seven years ago during undergraduate years on the campus of St. George's University, Grenada, where I was inspired by certain events that occurred in my life and that of my close friends. I thought it important at the time to put into writing some of the feelings that can never be spoken out loud or what the heart was feeling, but wanted to hide.

It was also a way of building a collection of work that I hopefully thought I would be brave enough to share someday; baring my soul. The emotions experienced were transferred into some of the varying pieces contained within this book, such as those on the notion of love and heartbreak- some of the very first works. Other pieces were penned over the last two years, 2014-2016 as my life evolved.

As a passionate individual, strong expressions are evoked, and life given to feelings and associations. I have used the gift of writing as an avenue to share significant issues that one might be faced with in real life, such as that of pain and loss, seeking direction, distrust, acceptance of self/diversity and other. Then, there are those moments of finding peace and enjoying life around us through our surroundings and spiritual experiences. All these and more are interwoven in one or two of the pieces within this collection, solely for your enjoyment.

I would like to express my gratitude to Heather Gillard for believing in me and cheering me on. Thank you Janet for the positive encouragement and for my love of books. To my Mom, thank you for all of your hard work and prayers.

Echoes of a broken heart

It seems like yesterday when the door closed on us
We both went our separate ways
The endless torture that plagues my mind
Keeps me in constant solace
The price I have paid for love
That unknown, obscured concept
My heart is tender, bruised, at odds with my mind
I thought I had let go….
I thought that I was immovable…..
That no longer will I remain vulnerable at any one's door
Nights of weeping
Blaming circumstances, I have sustained
My heart has bled a thousand times over
I thought I would remain immune until I met you

I tried hiding myself in the comfort of my own embrace;
Sheltering myself from the negative forces of this world
But I was wrong
I am affected
I am scared
Please show me how to trust again
How to make myself believe once more
My mind and heart is willing

Light Bulb

I never knew that being apart from
someone for even just like one day
Can seem like a thousand years
When I saw you today
My mind and every fiber of my being
was attuned to your magnetism
I just wanted you to know that my
sentiments are indeed sincere

Fade

It assaulted my senses
Filling me with intense longing
Nostalgia is potent
O my lips being kissed gently
Butterflies fluttering
I remember your embrace
Your voice whispering honey -soaked words
I am taken back to clandestine moments
Memories of well spent times together
Forever embedded in my heart
Days have flown on the stern of a sailboat
Months have collided and time stands still
Am I to forever bask in loneliness?
Reminisce about the past bliss?
My heart is playing the chords of the guitar
The strum of the violin
It beats faster and faster
It stops, it slows to the waltz
The sounds are fading in my ear
I strain to catch a whisper
I move slowly, my feet shuffling
I can no longer keep abreast of my sluggishness
I am tired
You have played out your tunes

I am in a desolate place
Tears slip gentle down my face
Everything is blotted
Forever concealed in dreams
Everything fades, fades fades

Play Me

I am your instrument
Shiny, brand-new and fine-tuned
I sing you sweet songs
Songs that resound from my heart
My lips sing you praises
My body is ripe and beareth luscious fruits
Bite me
Suckle me,
Inhale my sweet fragrance
Get lost in the intoxicating, arresting sounds of my soul
Caress and treasure me
I am your guitar

Your violin,
Your piano,
Your trumpet,
Your saxophone
Play on

What more can I give?

It always seems as if I put myself out for disappointment
No matter how much you try to show or
to explain with words, actions-
How much you care-
It appears futile
How much more can I take?
How much more can I give?
I have tried to show you
You know my feelings
You tangle my mind with weeds
And weave your cobwebs of disguise
What shall I hold onto?
Time after time I have put myself on the shelf for you-
Even when I thought that the shelf
was fragile-made of glass
Broken, crumbling at your feet
Shattered beyond repair
Sparkling like thousands of gems in the sunlight
Only for you to hold, admire-your only treasure
A find so rare
You seemed confused
Your mind is shadowed with distant fog
Can't you see clearly?
What more do you want?

You said we were two stars crossed from the beginning
We were magnets propelled since the beginning of time
Can't we cross that ocean?
It does not have to be a barrier
I cannot for one second settle my thoughts-
They are filled with you-your image, our talks
It's hard
It seems insane
Why can't it be simple for us?
I wonder if we will meet in the end
But for right now it is painful to think we would not
The same scene replays in my head
I can see us, I dream us, and I want us
It hurts, yes it is mind confusing
You know, I know
But we leave it up to time
Maybe destiny will play out in the end as it
was meant to be from the beginning!!

LOVE ME

He is to be different
Yes, not like all the rest hooligans
Hiding behind the façade of gentlemen
He is supposed to hold my hand
Not hit me as wanting to leave a brand

Respect me he must
For all I believe in and trust
We can differ on opinions and have
different ways of doing things
Romance is expected now and then
Let me feel like a princess

Yes. Give me sweet kisses
Wine and dine me
Remember my birthday
Our first kiss
When we fell in love

Some flowers will do
Will remind me that your sentiments are true
Be my friend to the bitter end
Tell me your fears
Dreams or the impossible
Hear me out
Comfort and cherish me
When I don't make it
Lend me your shoulder
Yes, be my strong tower and boulder

Tell your friends the whole world about us
Do not hide and seek nor be ashamed of me
Love me and my insecurities
All I want is to be perfect for you
Let the moon stars and sun reflect in your eyes
When you gaze upon my countenance

Excuse me if I want you for myself
My love knows no limit
I will respect your space

Don't vanish without a trace
Just be yourself, you have nothing to prove
I will love you for you
Just as long as you love me for me
Do not expect me to change or be someone else
I can only be me
Just me
Love me
Only for me

Betrayed

Pain, slain, in vain
No Gain
Crash, slash, bash
Across my heart
Flutters, thud, melted
Heightened, slammed, jammed
Dazed, hazed, in a maze
Blinded, frustration welled
Disappointed to the core
Speech cannot explain
Branded, wounded
Open, broken, left unsealed
Bled, left to die

State of Mind

It seems just like yesterday since I met you
Your bold eyes captivated me from the start
You said hello and I was forever lost
In your intoxicating world

Three weeks can stretch into a year
Yet I cannot tire of your wittiness
Your intellectual mind is one to be astounded by

Your zest for life is amazing
Your subtle remarks I cannot get enough of
I have drank and fed off every breath you breathe

You are leaving
I am filled with gloom
I will miss you
My heart is heavy
All I do is close my eyes and reminisce
I shall not forget
Forever shall I hold in my heart
The treasures that I have found
Dreams torments my state of mind
Forever you'll be mine

Colourful passion

I am soaked in diversity
Cloaked in mystery
my passion runs red
I can be compared to the sleekness of a tiger
Fascinating, beautiful, intensifying
I am full of life- brimming to the top
Overflowing with love and wonder
Full of excitement, colour, laughter
Yes I'm a prism
Reflecting light in radiance
I burn with fervor
An all-consuming flame
Passionate, charismatic
Oh that's me, that woman of fame

Dreams

I awoke from dreams of you
in the thick of the night
with the waves high
and the wind whistling at my door
and the moon's shining light cascades over
mountains, villages and streams
Illuminating all below
And the crickets and cicadas hidden in the depths
Chorused in harmony- A musical
crescendo graced the night

Nature has created this moment
where hearts, thoughts and passion collides
when at last the fire inside has been vented, then subsides
No more craving delights
I awoke from dreams of you

DIVERSITY

We are meant to be different
Have complex natures
We clothe ourselves in many layers
multichromatic facets of life represented

Chinese, Americans, Caribbean
Differing perspectives
Mannerism unique to all
Speech well defined
colour doesn't matter
Race is not an issue

Are we one?
Are we not flesh?
Our blood runs red
Cut us open; we bleed the same

what separates us?
Barriers?
Break them down
No separation
love, respect

As the birds we are meant to be free
Soar and we will see

What is love?

Love is deep
Love is magical
Love is pure
Love is phenomenal

Love is being sentimental
Love is saying you are sorry
Love puts up no barriers
Love destroyeth not
Love is love
Love is wise
Love is lovely
Love is beautiful

when you love
You love
When you fall in love
You are over the moon

When you fall out of love
You are forever scarred
Barriers erected

THEN Love will no longer be: deep, magical,
pure, phenomenal, sentimental, nor Lovely
BUT Love is remarkable
over the top
Vivid and
Exquisite!!

Absent

Why me? Why me?
These are the words her lonely soul pleads.
Her life is filled with so much heartache and pain.
Surrounded by loved ones who are
happy, constantly smiling
Laughter filling their days, carefree to enjoy life

Who is she?
Who is this person that has invaded her body,
stolen her thoughts, her every waking moment?
She's absent from herself
Her life drags on day after day
The future looks dismal

Birds sing their lovely melody in the air
Trees slowly blossom
Babies are being born into this world,
taking their first breath
BUT she is like an empty void needing to be filled
Anguished at the thought of never finding love

I do not want to be absent! Oh please
not me! Her lonely heart pleas.

Chance Meeting

I met you on a warm August evening
It was a chance meeting
I admired your black, thick crop of hair as it glistened
And a lock or two feathered your forehead
In your ear were two studs that enhanced your looks
You had warm, brown, bold, intelligent eyes
They mirrored years of wisdom surpassing your generation

You were sweating over the open grill
Concentrating at your task
I approached, complimented you
You were warm, open and true

From right there I saw your heart come to the forefront
Your voice was gentle with highlights of curiosity
Strange enough, I felt like I had known you longer

You opened up a dam in me
That flowed languidly
You offered a drink and that I accepted hesitantly
But eventually you spoke of poetry-
Captivated my interest

I wanted to know more then and there
I was hungry for spoken words
But I guess my time was up
How could I tap all the water at the same time?

I received your poem
You kind man
My interest was sparked
I responded in glee
My heart almost came apart
I hungrily ate all the words

Laughing, my friends thought I was insane
My fingers flew over the keys
Sending you one of my own piece
I entitled the subject of the email:
'Barbecue: Chance Meeting'

I have gotten to know you through your work
Your emotions, expressions, associations
Were penned in every line you wrote
I was awed by the feelings and depth
that poured out of your soul
You are amazing
I am glad we had that chance meeting

Passion

A caress
A moan
A flutter of butterfly wings
Sweet music orchestrated
Hands wondered
Without direction
Unsure of destination
Trailed aimlessly
A maiden of uncertainty
Denies the calling of passion

Chemistry ignited
Ecstasy inevitable
Attuned to the motions
Feelings and molecules of each other
Senses overwhelmed
Heights attainable
Almost there
Crashes
Moment suspended
Calms

Love Torn Tragedy: What If?

What if the sky turns red?
What if the moon stops shining?
What if the trees stop bearing fruits?
What if the oceans turn black?
What if we were meant to be together?
What if our hearts beat as one?
What if we deny our desires?
What if fate decreases our chance of a happy ending?
What if angels appear to us?
What if life was all that simple?
What if we are never given a second chance?
What if we go our separate ways?
What if I strongly desire you, love you, and want you?
What if circumstances prevents us
from achieving greatness?
What will we do?
What if we are soulmates?
What if we can make it work?
What if we can forget our pasts-shape the future?
Let's stop living this dream
Make it reality
Search deeply
It may produce certainty
Surely not probability

Windows to the soul

Looking into the mirror
A reflection so intense
Eyes squinting
Glanced rapidly from side to side
Years of hard toil reflected in those opaque windows

Exhausted
Drooping shoulders
Wondering what the next day will bring
Bowed over with the pains, agonies,
past mistakes, present situation
Shivers foretell someone walking on my grave
Shaking myself to awareness
A new day to contemplate upon flowers

Erika: Ode to Dominica

Erika oye-
Is why you so?
Erika oye-
Why you crept over us like that?
Erika: you knew we were not expecting
you to destroy us so,
But you left your backside (*rump*) outdoor.

Erika:
Granny did say that you were a bad girl,
Erika:
You know what, she was correct!
Your intense crying for hours upon
hours way up in the sky;
Your tears collected in our rivers,
Majestic mountains and streams.

Erika oye-
Is why you so?
Erika oye-

All for what?
Well, we came to a theory you know,
Yes Erika!
We said that your boyfriend Danny, that
came over us the week before,
Left running from way up East and
travelled down North without you-
He left a trail of weather that you became upset about;
Because it obstructed your path.
Erika oye-
Is why you so?
Erika oye-

Yes, You!
Don't be coy now Erika after you left us in ruins-
You wept without mercy and still did not let up,
You found our Nature Isle to be comforting-
Because of our soothing mountains:
Lush vegetation and tranquil waters,
So you remain above us.
Erika oye-
Is why you so?
Erika oye-

You took away defenses, bridges, airports, our homes;
BUT what caused us pain Erika-
Is the fact that you took so many lives-
Over 30 were dead or gone,
The unsettling devastation you left in your wake,
Caused much heartache.
Erika oye-
Is why you so?
Erika oye-

We still have not gotten over you,
Because we know for sure what you did was true,
Our Island stands testimony to this-
People are no longer in sweet bliss-
Now with every passing cloud,
With every single rain drop;
Panic ensues and pins can be heard if dropped.
Erika oye-
Is why you so?
Erika oye-

We are now getting back on our feet,
But still inside we weep.
You have etched your markings in our proud mountains,
It is unbelievable that once roaring
rivers now trickle like fountains.

Erika oye-
Is why you so?
Erika oye-

It is unsettling how times have changed-
As you were an historic storm-
We never expected you to happen like that;
But, from now Erika, we are watching our backs!
Times are changing everywhere,
Weather patterns unpredictable;
We say its climate change,
But man must shoulder some blame!
We continue to destroy Mother Nature-
Mother earth is crying out-
Pleading, angry at the mouth.
Erika oye-
You've taught us well
Erika oye-

Rest assured we are indeed building back-
Ten times stronger and that is a fact!
It is going to take over 20 years,
But from you, we have learnt to face so many fears.
Erika oye-
You've taught us well
Erika oye-

It is ironic how you were a blessing in disguise
Some say a curse,
But let nature speak-
Let nature roar its fury through our rivers-
Our pride,
Our joy;
That precious resource we seem to take for granted.
Erika oye-
You've taught us well
Erika oye-
I am sure that many lessons have been learnt,
And with pride and dignity:
And reverence,
Yes, and humility too,
We bow at our knees-
Giving thanks for our blessings;
Now we must get up and move mountains
Yes! Rejoice in living!
It is time for healing- uniting and reflecting.
Erika oye-
You've taught us well
Erika oye-

Erika oye-
Girl we wish you well,
But please, next time,
Warn us well!!!

Dominica is a small island found in the Caribbean, West-Indies. It has been named the "Nature Isle of the Caribbean" for its unspoiled natural beauty. It lies south-southeast of the French Islands, Guadeloupe and northwest of Martinique. The Island was devastated by tropical storm, Erika in August of 2015. This poem pays tribute to the people of the Island.

Glory Day

It arrived on the back of a stud horse
The rider slowly gaining momentum as
he charged across the plateau
He was chased by pelting fat bold raindrops
That cascaded from the once blue sky-
Now black, angry and growling
All around him was shrouded in a cloak of deception
He urged his horse onwards into the dense vault
Mud splattered everywhere

The trees in the distance
Slowly bowed their heads in worship as
the rain glided over their branches
Nature wept unmercifully for the days that
had gone by with dry unquenchable thirst
Birds swooped and dipped their wings in
salutation of such a spectacular display

The rider pressed his jodhpurs into the flanks of the horse
He was drenched to the bone
His only hope was to reach the sanctuary
of trees in the near distance
His horse weary from exhaustion

Skidded from side to side in desperation
The rider angled his body in preparation
For a non-graceful fall

Then all of a sudden the rain stopped
The sun peeked its head from among the parting of clouds
It sent forth its rays that shone like
a prism through the trees

The rider raised his head expecting his fall
But the horse braked
He held tightly to the reins
He did reach the sanctuary of the trees
He smiled because he knew he had endured it all

Journey

From the moment of conception to the time of birth
A map has been plotted
It's like a sailor mapping the course
to be taken for his voyage
Our lives have many courses to take
Numerous times we would have tried to avoid
the twists and treacherous paths to be taken
Then there are times when the trenches
and potholes cannot be avoided
They appear for a reason
What will you do when they are met?

We spend our lives dreaming of
something we want to accomplish
Sometimes we may fail no matter how much we try
It then becomes hard to understand
Or even hard to swallow
Persistence may drive us to take a different
route the next given opportunity
Then there are times we are meant to
follow a route not mapped out by us
Maybe a higher being is in control of your life's path

Can't you see that our lives do not belong to us?
Consider the journey
Your journey in life
What are you doing to make it successful?
What have you done to slow it down?
Is your path narrow, wide, smooth or rough?
Where will this journey lead?
Do you know?
Have you for once considered that the course
plotted that you think is perfect
May well turn out to be the journey
that can lead to failure
Sometimes in life, with some things
We cannot just decide the outcomes
Should we then leave our paths to be
taken in life up to fate or faith?
You decide
Consider, how many journeys are to be taken in your life?
Will it be one or several?

Nature's Fury Part 1

A fiery dragon came to life
It unfurled its fang in all directions
It roared from deep within the cave of Blacksand
Spitting fat droplets of raindrops and
pelting the land with spears

The wind in retaliation
Said, "No dragon,
I will take back precedent over this land"
She howled in protest
Letting up a cyclonic motion- a vacuum
sucking everything in its path

The ocean turned misty
A blanket of tears created
Crying for nature's unleashed fury

She danced the merengue
The salsa
The calypso
The sound of confusion plagued this
wretched, God forsaken place
Birds against the sobbing skies
Frightened out of their black feathery coats
Hustled east not knowing where to go

NATURE'S GLORY PART 2

To experience nature in all of its glory
The winds so strong
Waves so rough
Coconut trees limboed,
Their arms out stretched
Swinging wildly in the breeze

There, stood amidst this wild, amazing tribute to nature
Arms braced on hips
Swaying with the wind
Drenched and excited
Face heavenward
Rejoicing in the moment of chaos

One by one friends came to witness
this spectacular experience
People asked: "Are you crazy?"
Yes! I'm drunk off nature in its wildness/ fury and glory
It beckoned, so wanted to be part of it.
'Twas amazing
I felt revitalized and euphoric!!!!!

No longer able to keep up with the race
Dragon went back to space
As for the wind, she smiled
Then went somewhere to hide
The ocean relaxed
The trees in reverence bowed their dewy heads-
Tears slipping down their faces
Thankful for nature's unfurled fury

Exalt

Emotions are potent
We cry
We sing praises unto his name
We encourage
We abide
We must pray on our knees
We must lift each other up
There is no problem too big
No mountain too high
We must invite him into our lives
Let our bodies be purified temples
We must be clean vessels-
Let him dwell
We must be ready to bow down
He is the master of it all
We must lay our burdens at his feet
We must pray one for another
He loves us
Cherishes us
Let us-
Let us embrace him
Let us-
Let us tell someone of his love
Lord you are mighty and above all

Meditation

A solitude figure on the rocks looked towards the horizon
embracing the cold, yet soothing, fresh morning breeze
At peace with the surroundings

The rocks, big mossy eroded statues were
a comfort to black, creepy crabs
The stillness of the morning echoed the silence of thoughts
Waves glided towards the rocks
swished, swashed, plopped, held for a moment in suspense
Their frothy layers leaving swirls behind

Transfixed by this phenomenon
Questions bombarded the mind
God and his creation
Glad to be part of it

This morning I really appreciated the value of life
So many wonders,
Senses to observe
Attuned with the ocean
life and my thoughts

Flowers for a Lady

A handpicked bouquet of flowers was brought to me
Such delight was derived from the sight
Red, Pink, Yellow
Not one was blight

The sweet honeysuckle pervaded the air
And brought me good cheer
This sentiment shown from a friend
Was one to be treasured to the very end

I stuck a delicate petal in my hair
Walked around as an ostrich putting on air
At last they became wilted
Losing their precious petals
But this gift of flowers
Meant so much than diamond, gold or dollars

Late Nights

The worms in our stomachs growled
Rumbled like thunder
We were up studying-
Decided we couldn't take it much longer

Out to the kitchen Lisa go
I asked how she was moving so slow
She salvaged some chicken and rice
And cooked up a 1:30 pot real nice

Into our rooms we went
Lana came in and did the same
She scrambled eggs and bacon too
What ah full plate when she got through?

Lisa went back for a second portion
I chewed and swallowed in slow motion
These late night pots
Oh what ah blessing
Studying at SGU wasn't any easy thing
Still we have to give thanks
I just hope we can wake up for class in the morning!

Subliminal

Silence echoes empty thoughts
Dreams surfaced in our minds
Forever transported to a different realm

Bruised
Torn
Covered in mud
Ants crawled on mossy leaves
A new day has dawned
A dark cavern unfolds its treasures

Second Chances

Around the outer edge of the square
There is still a glimmer of hope
To go tumbling off the brink into
nothingness is frightening
Being hopeless
Trapped and foolhardy

Life is precious
Meant to be embraced
Go out there
Hit sixes
Believe in everything good
You are given a second chance
Impact

Nonsense Poems

Rain
Hobble squibble squabble
Rain dribbled
Created a babble
Rumble tumble straight into the puddle
singing splashing making a muddle
Childhood frolicking
Wonderful troubles in the making

Rain
Dribble hobble squabble
Babble rabble tallow
Sable cabble shallow
Sing swim fish in the puddle
Childhood frolicking

Rain

Fat cold raindrops
Fell from the sky
A mop of tears

Dinky the Bat

Dinky the colourful bat
One day dropped his hat
He flew vigorously down the meadow
Met old spiky Rover sitting on his seadow
Made a keening scream
Woke a young panther from his dream
Startled the curious llama
Searching all over for his mama
That ill-mannered, temperamental, inconsiderate bat

The vagabond cat

The old vagabond cat
Chased mercilessly after the hat
But the wind let up a storm
To no avail he chased the hat
That vagabond cat

Life

Life can give YOU a kick in the rear at times
Life can cause pain
Life can cause distress

Hmmm …people disappoint you
They forsake you
What else can they do?
Everything imaginable!!!!!

Well …I am taking it back
I am putting it back together
I am going to take full control
Oh yeah!!!
The feeling
This feeling
LIFE
You are in control!!!!!!!!!!!!!!!!

Pain

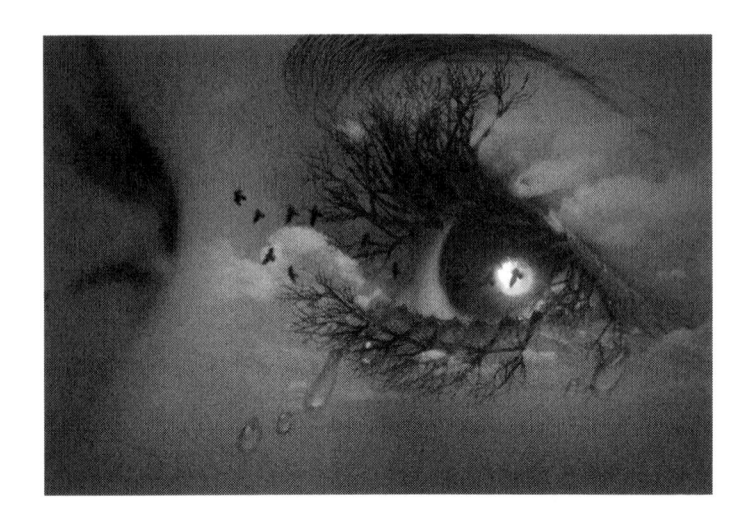

Pain- that ugly emotion that steals your breath
That gruesome beast that insists on rearing its ugly head
That enemy in the room breathing
down your neck with foul breath
The slashing of the warrior's sword
The clamming of sweaty palms against your body
The white blinding lights behind closed eyelids
Meant to block the intrusion of reality
Pain reveals its nature in the intensity that sears the soul
It concentrates on attacking that part
of the body it has been told
Is it the head, legs, eyes, stomach or toes?

Oh yes! Pain claims your sanity and takes control
Pain does not discriminate
Old- young, pretty, ugly, rich
It does not matter if you are eight!!
Your status and social standing provides no shade
When pain comes knocking at your door
You must yield-
It is a leveling playing field
Some are stronger, hence gateways can cope
Others weaker, take drugs hoping to act as dope
We remember pain as a fleeting moment in time
As we overcome
It is yesteryears memory
Having gone through
Been through and can testify
The raging hands of the demon raging fire
BUT we have lived and can testify
That the hands that which tried to claim
Could not touch the Lord's sanctified!

Black Is My Beauty

What makes me different from them?
Is it my hair, colour or structure?
Is it the way I walk?
The way I talk?
Is my accent not refined?
Aren't my features captivating enough?
Is not the curve of my thighs just right?
Or the muscles in my legs tight?

Is it because I am black?
Is it because my culture is different from yours?
Is it what I do?
Tell me, what makes them better than me?
What can you possibly see?-
When you look at me?
Is it that they are of refined pasteurized milk?
Strands of corn silk in abundance?

What of uniqueness?
Can't you see?
Don't you know?
Aren't we connected?
Share similar passions, interests?
I cannot for once see the perplexity of it all!

Aren't you conscious of the fact that this is not superficial?
This is the entire package you see
When you look at me
A strong black beauty

Well ….I will take my uniqueness
Pack it up
Sealed from the outside
Blast karma… fate
Or whatever we say
I will make my impact in this world
I will not define myself for anyone
I will not dodge my beliefs
Neither will I pretend nor hide
I will be me
A strong Nubian goddess
Yes, I am black, proud and beautiful
If only you could see!
BLACK is my beauty!!

My Room

There is a place where I can go hide from the world
My thoughts bounces off its walls
I can vent my frustration in my comfy pillows
When I am cold
My loving comforter offers open arms
I can snuggle

My room never rejects me
She sighs when she thinks the world has been harsh to me
Her walls reflects the look in my eyes
They tell no lies
Sometimes, I wish they would stop
being faithful and lie to me
Show me as a monster when I am angry
Show me as short when I don't want to be tall
Show me as being fashionable decked when am in rags
Or even show me as Cinderella awaiting her prince
When I am dreaming within her walls
BUT I love you for not doing those things
You are faithful and true

I love my room for her windows
They reflect the sunlight in all of its radiance
I am awoken to the sun rising

Or go to bed with the moon out.
My windows gives me a glimpse into
the dark world of pain/sorrow
It also closes when it becomes too harsh to bear
It protects me from the monsters wanting to
climb into my sanctuary; my fortress
It shields the destructive elements of nature
It remains a battle warrior

My room is proud to bear the
frustrations, battle cries, laughter
Even the intrusion of others known as friends
She loves me and has withstood time
Has passed from one generation within the family-
Now mine
I will not trade my place of fantasies,
nightmares, even solace
She loves me and I completely adore her faithfulness.

Ballad: Rosie's Demise [AH HUH]

This ballad speaks about a young girl named Rosie. Rosie was caught by her mother sneaking out of their home. Rosie after being admonished that her dad will basically chastise her if he knew, decided to still leave the house. Her worried mom stayed up waiting for her. She was so mad that she RANTED at her daughter when she came home. Rosie then told her angry mother that her attempts at punishing her was useless because she was pregnant and it was a matter of time before it came out. This was written for fun after undertaking a literature class in undergrad.

Rosie a skinny young 'gal'
Was caught sneaking out the house by her mother Etal
She said she was going to Spring Garden
Because her boyfriend Roderick wanted some closure
On a very important matter

Rosie, Dear, what is the matter?
Ah huh
You have no regards for your stature
At least hold up your character
Your father if he ever knew
Will surely give you a fracture

Rosie not wanting to listen
Cursed her mother and said she will be back
She took up her bag and was gone in a flash,
Ah huh
In her red mini skirt riding up her thighs
Leaving all to entice

Etal did not know what to do
Said she will give her a curfew
She sat in the dark to wait for her daughter
She did not know what minute nor hour,
Ah huh

Rosie came in around two
Her face looking all blue
Her clothes was in a mess
Her vest riding up on her chest
She closed the door quiet quiet
Thinking no one would know
But poor thing her mother was right there
Sat on two pillows,
Ah huh

Etal jumped in front of her
Deflating the wind in Rosie's tyre
Commanded her to sit in a chair
Jeez child, look what you putting me through?

Staying up waiting these hours for you
Girl, what I really want to do
The police will have to ensue,
Ah huh
From now on you on a ban
You are messing around with someone?
What do you want out of life?

Mother it is too late
I am setting everything on the plate
I found out that I am in a mess
I want everything off my chest
So why rave and shout
The damage has been done and would come out,
Ah huh

Etal opened her mouth very wide
Wanting to talk but the tide subside
She clearly was in shock
Dropped on her two knees and started to rock
Rosie then got scared
Started to shed crocodile tears
She said: "Mother what I will do now?
I am going to look like a sow!!"!
Ah hu- ah- huh
Ah- huh, Ah- huh, Ah-huh

Island Life

Rain
Hammering against the thin galvanized roof
Wishing for a genie
To eliminate the sounds with a poof

Roasted breadfruit
And stewed chicken
Rice and peas
Fried Jack fish
Dukunah, corn pie, callaloo soup
These are just some of the foods
That will get us through

Waking early mornings to go to school
Consoled by Momma's wisdom:
Use education as an important tool

Oh the days of sweet vacation
Spending time with Grandma
Going fishing in the river
Catching crayfish
Sometimes lobster
Making a tasty meal
With green banana

Climbing mango trees to sample the fruits
Playing cricket, dodge and marbles in the road
Getting in trouble for stealing a treat
Dancing to the drums
Not missing a beat

Running everywhere
With our bare feet
Mischievously lighting fires
To feel the heat

Taking water from standpipes
To fill up the drums
Life was much peaceful then without the threat of guns
Life was much peaceful then without the threat of guns

Oh Island in the sun
Oh my sweet paradise
Oh the memories I have of you
You have indeed birthed a daughter so true!

The End of the Road

It seems like yesterday I was a child
Playing, frolicking, crying, clinging
Now my childhood days are over
Those days filled with bittersweet memories

It was just yesterday I was a teenager
A beauty to behold
Entice, swayed, insecure
Too many decisions to make
Those moments then are ones I shall treasure

Today, I am a woman grown
Capable of making sure decisions

Can deal with my insecurities
Confident in my beliefs
Would have done my best to attain my goals

I have a life filled with purpose
I know where I am
Where I want to be
Now, today at the present moment
I have accomplished many feats
Uprooted barriers in my path
Extended my range

I am a success story
A story if to be told
Will reveal pain, sadness, doubt, and heartache
But today, I can say I have maximized my
strengths and those of loved ones
I can say without a doubt
That I have overcome several chapters of my life
These chapters constitute many pages
Turn a page and you will find
How one woman moved everything
To accomplish greatness
AND is still moving forward
Rising on Eagle's wings

The End

Printed in Great Britain
by Amazon